Lee Rodin

Y0-AHG-401

Alzina Mayo

Tapestry

# of a Soul

.....Out of man's lowest tide arises his highest self.....As personal comforts and physical pleasures disappear, we search. The avenue of that search is of extreme importance.

THE ARIES PRESS PO BOX 30081
CHICAGO, IL 60630

© 1980 The Aries Press

ISBN 0-933646-13-5

Publisher
        The Aries Press
        P.O. Box 30081
        Chicago, IL 60630

All rights reserved. No part of this book may be reproduced in any manner whatsoever without the written permission of the publisher.

Printed in the United States of America

Typesetting by Constance DeMarco

Production by Tom O'Connor

About the Authoress

Alzina M. Mayo is the founder and president of the House of Magic Numbers and is a working numerologist for more than fifteen years. She is the mother of five children, a native of Indiana, and travels extensively both at home and abroad lecturing, teaching, and doing regular radio and TV appearances. Alzina is now recognized as an international numerologist working in all but three countries of the world.

In Preparation
by
Alzina Mayo

Chronicle of a Working Numerologist

With the Turn of a Card

About this Book

The book you are about to read is about the philosophy she uses behind her numerology work.
She makes the statement that numbers without philosophy are dead and that we must teach people how, through their attitude, to make life better.

The unicorn has portrayed a mystical beauty throughout the ages. Connections between man's bondage to earth and his spirituality are apparent. His body is set firm on earth and yet released by his spiritual awareness. Although meant to deal with earth environment, he depends greatly upon universal direction. It is as if the Christ nature of man is exemplified by the horn swirling in the form of a receptive "divining" rod. The Christ Spirit is always felt as a pulsating force. The countenance of his nature is serene strength and spirit---
what better image to use for this work than the Christ spirit.

Contents

- I   The Quest   9
- II   What of Man's Purpose in Life?   11
- III   Fear   15
- IV   Hate   19
- V   Pride   21
- VI   Jealousy   23
- VII   Depression   27
- VIII   Greed, Envy   29
- IX   Our Second Crystal   31
- X   Truth   33
- XI   Love   37
- XII   Growth of the Soul   41
- XIII   Faith, Hope   45
- XIV   Real Beauty   47
- XV   Love Consciousness   49

Preface

It has often been said that out of man's lowest tide arises his highest self. The most spiritual works in history have come pouring forth in this fashion. Personal tragedies and wars seem to have this effect upon mankind. When our outer image and securities are stripped away we go within. As personal comforts and physical pleasures disappear, we search. The avenue of that search is of extreme importance. Of those who choose to search inwardly, their higher self bursts forth.

War truly manifested the wisdom and leadership of Winston Churchill. The genius of his remarkable speeches moved others forward. When England was at the point of defeat and disaster, this man's voice and inspiration turned it to victory. William Shakespeare's works were done in less than affluence, but still live. The brainchild of Shakespeare still today teaches depth and understanding of human nature.

The beginnings and the beliefs of every religion started with one man's inspiration from the universe. One man's understanding about God consciousness. The list is endless and reads like a Hall of Fame register. They appear as lights throughout the political, religious and literary circles.

I think on these things as I hear individuals pleading for release from a defeating experience. The phrase "defeating experience" is a flexible subject depending totally upon the individual. What seems normal and standard to us may be another's trial. Your personal testing-ground may be a difficult marriage, a struggle with children, pressures of career, financial strain, or a physical weakness. We all have at one point in our lives encountered one of these situations. Whatever your personal upheaval, it may be your lowest tide. The reasons or persons behind your point of truth are of little importance. Just the fact that you are at that low ebb is the challenge. Will you, at this point, reach inward or outward? The direction is the assurance of success or failure. As a soul at this point of crisis reaches inward to the universe, greatness comes. The universe holds the same abundance of quality for us all. Your mental I.Q., large or small, has very little to add. It may color the language or polish the word stones to be more pleasing. The knowledge offered is the greatness, no matter what the form. The force and flow you obtain is stable, sure, and infallible.

   The work you are about to share was accomplished at the lowest ebb of my life. A looming mountain of the most defeating experiences was present. A witch's brew consisting of a troubled marriage, five small children, financial problems, physical weakness, and self-image doubts. Perhaps the most defacing of these being the unhappiness with my own image and self-esteem. This manuscript came pouring forth in the midst of that depressing combination of affairs. That higher mind we all possess heeds not temporary conditions or attitudes. This set of circumstances and the reaching inward happened eleven years ago. Knowing things were truth did not change the situation of my life instantly; however, my mind changed and I viewed all things differently. Slowly....over the next few years my life did change. This was accomplished by my thoughts leading my whole world into clearer vision. Our outward world will conform to our inner whole self in growth. Through the years the understanding and help it has given me has been priceless. Just to glance back over it gave me the power to continue. Year after year, I can truly say it has been a comforter.

You will find nothing new in this book for the statements here are as old as time, but still are sound. If you have just begun your search for answers, it may help. This could be the frame you need truth mounted in, to accept and use it. Now I have found the courage to share its content with others. You are therefore entrusted with that which is my best self. Hopefully, you will find it is your best self, also.

The first few chapters of this book may appear negative. Man, being as he is, must see darkness to distinguish light. There must be a display of the extreme negativity so we then will choose light. The difficulty in reading the negative is in identification. You will become aware of how much each negative phase has seeped into your life.

Digesting this whole context will take more than one trip through. Think of yourself as a science student as you ingest it fully. Read it in stages and discuss it with fellow seekers. You will have a rule of thumb to gauge

*your areas of growth. Remember,
as you approach the positive areas,
we are all possessed with that highest
Christ mind. This tapestry of oneness
is not only given to the greats, but
also to us. That magnificent work of art
is within us always. We have only to open
our inter-resources and let it flood
our lives.*

Chapter 1

Welcome to the Quest for Truth
and Answers. Our probe will reach
outward into the Universe
and inward to our Soul's depths.
These are questions we all ask
within our own Minds and Hearts.
 Let the words that follow singe
deep into your Inner Self. Let them
penetrate beyond Environment, Religion,
and Tradition---to the very Core
of your Being.
 Then listen....while the chords
of your Soul respond
in the clear tones of a bell.
 A lovely feeling of identification
warms the dark corners of remembrance.
Listen as my thoughts become
your thoughts. My questions
are the very ones you have pondered
in seeking Meaning for Life.
 Watch as piece after piece
of this mystery falls into a position
of understanding. We can use
this enlightenment and grow
from the knowledge.
 It is all so simple and so perfect.
We have stumbled over the simplicity---
intent upon making it difficult.
 Enter then into my Mind and Soul
as we seek and find the answers
to our Quest. The only requirement is

an Open Mind. Put your limitations away.
Put them away as a child's toy
and take up real Truth.
 Doors which have stayed firmly shut
will suddenly swing open. The only
closed doors are self-imposed,
so open the doors of your Mind
and free your mind's potential.

Chapter II

   I stood watching the falling leaves drift aimlessly across the extent of my view. They swayed, moving at random, tossed by the slightest breeze. A gust of wind set them into whirlwind patterns of confusion.
   No inner life motivates them and disorder appears their permanent lot. Definite directions of movement are impossible to maintain. They are completely reliant upon outside stimuli to produce energy.
   In the beginning they were an outward display of a growing, breathing and useful part of Nature's tapestry. Alive, responding, reacting....their presence added to the world's softness. Tenderness of touch was expressed through them to the world's senses. Beauty was an important part of their existence---giving off the fragrance of fresh new life.
   They had a definite position to fill in life's processes....theirs was an all-consuming task to accomplish. They fit precisely into the Rhythm Pattern of Nature.
   Their harmony with all of Creation's functions shows a unity. Soothing the world to rest at night and giving birth to each new day was their portion.... Purpose was the Key that unlocked the reason for Life.

Now with the removal of Life Purpose, death has set in. No reaction transpires within their ranks unless produced from outside influence. It seems to me a strange parallel exists here---a parallel between Man without Life Purpose and leaves ready for decay.

There are but two directions of change or movement in Nature's scheme of things. One direction is evolving upward and ever expanding, while the other direction is lifeless decay---giving back to earth matter for recycling.

Within us and about us operates a process of everything becoming something else. Nothing stays the same and all Creation moves toward one of these directional destinations.

Man, not being unique in nature's design, complies with these cycle directions. Growth and death cycles are designated by the presence or the absence of Life Purpose.

What of man's Purpose in life? Or perhaps a far better definition would be "man's Obsessions in life". We are told it is wrong, or evil, to be pushed and led by obsession.

Tradition submits the theory that total destruction will accompany this kind of driving force.

Is this electrical passion for a definite outcome of your life, wrong?

Is this force the reaper of degradation and misery?

Of course you realize this could be a false conclusion and far from the whole truth.

The fact is....obsession could be, in many applications, salvation to a seeking Inner Self.

To really understand the whole subject, we must take time to investigate, as misunderstanding runs rampant in the actual effects of this phenomena. Even more misunderstanding exists on the effects it exerts on human affairs.

To understand implies complete engrossment and encasement of a subject. To understand obsession, then, we must experience each positive....and negative aspect.

All that is a portion of the Cosmos....if dissected, is found to contain both negative and positive sections or poles.

As intelligent beings, it is for us to make the decisive plans for the best use of the Power. We can with the right motives make the best use of this or any other Power in our hands.

It would seem here that the positive or negative path is a decision to be made. We may choose from which direction we wish to exist and to operate.

This factor alone may be the most important decision of our life.

A complete analysis would seem the correct procedure to follow. We must be willing to explore the internal structure in deep degree, peering into each Life Purpose for the positive and negative atoms in operation there.

In truth---these Life Purposes, or Goals, are mysteriously powerful crystals. They embody and supply enormous amounts of energy and driving force.

Upon contact with a needed experience or knowledge, the process of osmosis is released. Thus the experience or knowledge actually becomes a part of us to be used in the achievement of our Life Purpose.

From this, then, we can assume obsession also contains a drawing power, as well as a driving power. The potential is there for the negative....and for the positive. Each of us must make that final decision as to which direction to take.

Let us go forward now to explore and to become engrossed in our research project.

Chapter III

Before us swings a crystal of the ultimate negativity. In the mind's eye we are aware of a strange intriguing beauty. It seems to possess the depth, highlights, and luster of a diamond. Is it any surprise the appeal this negative stone has for many? Upon first contact, its beauty is truly dazzling to the beholder. True characteristics are exposed only upon very close inspection. This is a poor imitation---a glass prism of negative facets. Under pressure, all of its power will crumble to dust. Fear is the real motivating force and power behind this false stone. The false prism has many flaws---all taking on the disguise of a precious stone. Upon close examination, we see a murky, red glare entirely covering the surface. It is clear that only destructive force operates within its realm. In smaller and smaller circles, this crystal spins into desperation and stagnation. At some far-off goal, only frustration will be found as a reward. Why? Because no soul growth has been accomplished. Here we have self-power seeking---not an obsession to enrich the soul. We now have need to enter each negative phase. We have no desire or wish to experience these emotions. Needless to say we have all fallen victim to these dark emotions. They are the scavengers of the universe at large. We know them by name---Depression, Desperation, Hate, Greed, False Pride,

Envy, Jealousy, Fear.

Keep in mind though, my friend, that Fear is the real motivation force behind the appearance of the other emotions. In fact, fear is the true Dr. Frankenstein of the negative attitudes of man. Should you doubt the truth of this statement, make a simple test. Make an honest appraisal of the real reason behind your own personal negative thinking. Remember the last time you gave yourself over to the deception of negativity....Be honest and search deeply into the hidden reasons. These reasons we hide from our own mind's conception---far back into the dusty corner of our souls. We guard them as some hidden treasure. What we actually guard with such vengeance is the forerunner of monstrous emotions. These negative emotions sap our energies and bring upon us the Death Cycle.

This crystal we are preparing to enter is a dark power prism. With expert precision, it deals the death blow to meaningful soul advancement. And so our probing research begins in earnest.

We step forward to face the first concept of the emotion of Fear. It is our wish to first understand the Seed Emotion of all negativity. Since this seething, snarling emotion gives rise to all the other negative thoughts, we first will experience and understand the cornerstone of all destruction. Slowly we approach the dark chamber of horrors---Fear's negative section. Once inside the mind is incapable of clear, logical thoughts. The ingredients used in this negative laboratory are self doubt, universal doubt, and even doubt in the God essence itself.

Fear is a black plague that produces disease and death of the soul. The order of each day is upheaval as the new negative thought enters and grows to maturity.

*This engrossment and negativity eventually
shows in our physical appearance. Our eyes
take on a hollow, unreal quality. They
look....but see nothing that is real.
All things, no matter how much beauty or
help they contain, are seen through
dark-colored glasses. Fear surrounds us
and holds us in a death grip. If any soul
advancement were offered, Fear would
quickly blot it out.
  We fear to live, we fear to try and---
most of all---we fear to fail. Each day
our fears mount and the fear of death
grows in strength. If we can be sure of
nothing in life, death strikes the most
desperate of fears in our heart. We hide
from all in life, fearing hurt at someone's
hands. We never, but never, reach out to
help another....we have nothing left with
which to help another. No reserve can
surface to extend and to comfort.
Encased in Fear's depths, we set ourselves
apart from all else. We make ourselves
the center of our own small universe.
The sun of our small, dark universe is
our own ego. It burns brighter and
brighter, dispelling all positive sparks.
In orbit around us are the negative aspects
of the Mind....Hate, Depression, Desperation,
Jealousy, False Pride, Greed, and Envy.
The very force of their pattern imprisons
us in our own negative world. At the
outer limits of our dark universe, the
positive aspects try to enter but,
unfortunately, the very force that holds
our negative solar system together will
exclude all positive....As time elapses,
our small world clusters---becoming
smaller and still smaller. Eventually
each negative emotion will destruct into
our own ego. This is the Law of the
Universal Bodies---to be drawn into the
center.*

Our ego is the sun and the center of our self-made world. Into this flaming ego we will eventually enter and be devoured. Nothing will remain in the space that once was ours---nothing will remain but complete utter darkness. No sound will be heard, no light will be seen, no movement will be exerted. We have been destroyed by our own negative power-crystal and action. Our cycle was the death cycle running frantically headlong to destruction. With understanding of the master emotion of the negative crystal, we retreat. We stop for a time, making sure that we are in true complete understanding of this facet.

We stand at a distance to scan the full range of Fear's operation. Our thoughts are disturbed by the effects that Fear exerts upon man. The man fully given over to Fear's domination seems helpless. He takes for a life-mate erratic mistrust. He fathers children of bitterness and hostility. His world is cold, hard, brutal, and without love. We shudder within, knowing that doom is awaiting final effort.

Fear

Chapter IV

We stand at the door of another entry into a regrettable frame of mind. Here at the door of Hate, reluctance urges us to turn aside. Flames of red shoot forth from the opening. The flames leap and reach angrily in all directions. We look deep into this blazing inferno to spot Fear's presence. There, deep in the midst of hate's flaming obverse, bursts forth the fear essence. Hate raises its serpent's head only when we fear some thing or someone. Its deadly venom flows relentlessly into our veins. Our mind is twisted in nightmarish dreams and thoughts. Images arise within our poisoned minds that haunt our dreams and plague our waking hours. Hate feeds from its own self....increasing in strength and vengeance. Always enlarging, it grows within our fevered brain. It coils tighter and tighter, crushing the very life from us. Again and again, it strikes its fatal blow sealing our fate. What started out as small and petty becomes a ravenous, entwining serpent. Our former idle toy ends by devouring us completely. Ugliness fills our days and loneliness fills our soul as the death rattle signals the approach of the end. We find ourselves alone for we have attacked all that once was friend. All that is left of our former selves is a snarling, hissing, venom-filled corpse. Our bones lie bleached by the sun and scattered by the winds of time. Finally, our bodies will be given back to earth for recycling.

There is a tremendous void within this facet which glares at us from inside. There is not a single sign of love, not a morsel of beauty is to be found, or is there a trace of truth to be found here....only pain, mistrust, and heartache pour forth in rivers of sadness. We find ourselves backing away from this concept of hate as not to touch its heart. We have found no useful emotion here. Instead we have found a glaring, deadly disease--- possibly the most contagious of all afflictions of man. The land of this affliction is a dry and barren desert. Within our minds and souls, the desert grows in size. The heat of the day is an inferno and the nights are icy cold. All is felt in raw, savage emotions. Rational thoughts fail to develop....all is colored by illusions. Here we shall end in a cycle of hate which never held any life-giving facets.

hate

Chapter V

The next negative aspect is impressive to the eye....the outside image is elegance in its highest form. This is the massive entrance to the stage of False Pride. A commanding position is assumed by this facet in our thoughts. We experience this negative concept only when we fear to be stripped of the camouflage we hold. Only when we fear to show our true selves does it appear. We feel a desperate struggle is in process here. The struggle is within one's self, tearing at every shred of beauty. Desperately we fight to keep our False Image intact. The hope is to cover any imperfection that may exist in us. We act out a part as well-rehearsed robots. We move without feeling as a puppet might. We are never late for a cue or curtain call. Pretense is all that remains alive and intact. Fearing to be ourselves, we cease to be at all. In fact we become as a shell filled with pretense and disguise.

We act out chosen roles but have ceased feeling the part. Each speaks his lines fluently, precisely, but hears no sound. We move with expert timing but fail to feel a response. Long have we played this charade, and worn a mask of deceit.

If all pretense was now removed, each would be formless....faceless. Each would be as the lifeless, hard scenery surrounding him. Emotions no longer flow to the surface of the face....it is frozen in a calm,

serene mold. All glow and radiance is
painted in place. Papier-mache makes up
the immediate world of response.

When life's audience responds with
approval, we live. Without the outside
applause, we are deadwood. We are dependent
upon outside opinion, outside response.
We search each face to be sure our secret
is safe. Fear mounts as the curtain
descends. Always we fear this will be
our last performance. Always the fear
of being found out. So, my friends,
we always live in fear....fear of the last
curtain call of life.

We feel the need for fresh air upon
leaving this negative section---breathing
deeply to rid ourselves of the feeling
of suffocation. Never could any part
of this facet serve a useful purpose.
Not even a definite color can be a sign
here....so vague is real emotion.

Pride

Chapter VI

We enter the next negative aspect with hesitation. Sounds of a tremendous battle emerges from its interior.

We experience a feeling of dread upon entering.

The color here is an ever-spreading cancerous dark green. Jealousy rises to do battle only when we fear our own inabilities.

Its war cry is a painful shriek warning the opposing forces of a declaration of arms.

Revenge seems to be the objective and the casualties are felled by the avenger's sword. His attacks are forceful and violent in nature. No pity is shown to the enemy, nor is there a trace of fair play.

Each campaign the avenger wins only gives grounds for yet another battle. Less and less reason is needed now to justify attack.

His steed is self-motivated by an inferiority feeling. The feeling of inadequacy lends yet more fury to his campaign.

His war tents spring up everywhere. No man is safe from his onslaught. Nothing is too sacred for his invading armies to crush.

No place is too far for his arm of revenge to travel.

Even his comrades-in-arms have long since become indispensable.
He can trust no man for he judges all against himself.
His war flags in procession conjure up dread and fear in the hearts of men.
He watches each engagement with satisfaction but never is his war done.
Never is he really satisfied.... always a new enemy is on the horizon.
Even his faithful lieutenants he has stripped of authority. One by one they have marched before the firing squad of his mind.
At each execution, he sat as supreme judge.
Now the end has come and he stands alone on his battlefield. No enemies are in sight....but no friends are in sight either.
Alone he shall stand....for he could trust no man and all became expendable.
This lone morbid figure surveys his victory field.
Somehow he feels not like the victor at all.
There is a hollow feeling to it and the spoils of war he collects is futility.
Limping forward across a wide valley, he sways with fatigue. He dares not close his eyes to sleep for fear of attack.
Scars of past battles are evident and painful.
Old wounds have a way of retaining painful memories to be relived over and over.

No more is his sword arm sure and steady to its mark. He pauses---trying to make some shred of sanity return to his fevered mind....but no---it's far too late for sanity's healing hand to help.

His mind refuses to comprehend reason and rejects true facts.

The sun flashes against his weapon as it slides to the ground. Bitter tears appear for surely he is the conquered, not the conqueror.

His defeat is complete as his war banner lies crumpled on the ground. Already the knowledge is haunting him.... already he knows the truth of the matter ---all his warring has not relieved his feeling of failure and uncertainty. Defeat of the innocent has not added one inch to his stature. A shudder runs through his frame as he realizes his time is spent.

A lone figure enters the field and rides slowly toward him. The rider is shrouded in black from head to foot. Even his horse of glistening white seems to understand the mission and moves with sure precision. His slate banner waves silently announcing his purpose.

He looks neither right nor left, but his eyes are fixed straight ahead.

A wave of relief runs through the crippled warrior as he watches the approach of
                death.
The final victory is assured always to the hooded figure of death.

With hollowness of soul, the weary victor of many wars accepts his fate.

Almost gladly he receives the way out
of his endless torment.
  He will now know peace for the
first time since jealousy became
his master.
  We close our eyes and turn away,
not wanting to see the final thrust.
A feeling of physical illness sweeps
over us and we flee this aspect.

Jealousy

Chapter VII

A grayish mist extends from the next phase of negative effects. Depression forms its solid wall of bleakness within this facet. Desperation operates and appears when we fear life holds nothing for us. We fear youth is slipping away and we have not yet lived. We feel no purpose in life is worth enduring life's insurmountable problems. With the foundation in the dark when problems and difficulties come, all is lost. There is no support to lean on, no truth to circle back and mend life's wounds. There is no growth to urge forward movement and forward seeking, no hope and faith to assure the answer is just ahead, no beauty to soften the blows of the world. Depression is a phantom which enters consciousness....a phantom of self-destruction and self-defeat. The mind is open to attack from the forces of desperation and despair. Thoughts of perceptiveness and objectivity lie silent and cold. Dark forces steal quietly into the main arteries of this miracle called Mind.

Tha phantom's armies spread like a plague affecting all we touch with fear and confusion. Our thoughts struggle desperately to gain a foothold from which to fight. He dredges up all the negativity in us and enlarges upon it. Depression's heavy hand reaches for our thought.... creating deep, dark cavities of hopelessness.

Mirrors are produced, focusing on only the worst of life....only the unpleasant parts and past mistakes are relived, including all heartaches. We are encircled by a wall of fear and loneliness. Our only thoughts are of self. The rise of this negative thought pattern has been in stages designed to camouflage its presence. It makes a cruel taskmaster for it demands the Soul. We are chained to its stockade of bleakness. Within the walls of this blockade, our cellmates are Jealousy, Hate, Suspicion, Fear, and Confusion. All of these fellow prisoners chant, "You are doomed, doomed....give in to the mundane in life."

We stand naked before the captor's glowing mockery. In circles we travel searching for an escape, searching for the key from our prison. The end results of depression are self-defeat, self-imprisonment, and self-destruction. One feels as if a reprieve has been offered upon leaving this facet.

No possible useful purpose can ever grow out of this kind of negativity. As we leave this phase of negative effect, we shake the dust from our sandals. The last thing we wish is to take any of these feelings with us.

Depression

Chapter VIII

Opening before us now are the colors yellow of greed and the dry browns of envy. These two are like ugly Siamese twins of negative birth---one must have the other to exist and live. All seems an essence of begrudging and of envy of others.
These dismal twins appear when we fear to have faith in the Universal powers. Fear that our wants and needs will not be supplied is at a fever pitch. In our estimation, all who are fortunate enough to have do not deserve to have. We judge all as unworthy to receive what we want. We become lost in panic, trying desperately to assure ourselves of tomorrow, and the process of today is lost and gone forever. Never will it be allowed to play its full part in our life. Our thoughts turn continually to worry. Worry for that which we must be prepared.
We conjure up images of exact positions in which we will need more than we have. We cannot concentrate on NOW because we are worried about tomorrow. Tomorrow isn't even here and no worry today can possibly add one ounce, or one inch, to tomorrow. If anything, worry will build negative thoughts in front of us. These thoughts grow in size and will circle back in a material aspect.
In other words, my friends, you can make the things you are worried about materialize

before you. You always feel your golden rainbow is off in the future. It never is the lovely free rainbow you expect.

If you could only treat today like an exciting page of life to be lived to the fullest, then each tomorrow would be a golden rainbow. How could it not be since today would be a very special day!

Our pot of gold in this facet is but a fairy gift that will surely fade. Each new day brings only grumbling, worry, and more procrastination. Fear has now expertly applied its stranglehold.

In this form and frame of mind, one cannot survive but will surely become as decayed leaves. Worry wrinkles will grow and freeze in place.

Greed and envy are the signposts we have chosen to follow. They will lead us down a long, dark path of desolation.

Having completed this negative phase of our research, we understand. We see Fear's full range of negativity when left unchecked. Fear, being a man-made emotion, is the real Dr. Frankenstein then.

Take these emotions, enlarge them billions of times, and we have the world condition....we see Fear, my friend, Fear in its most grotesque form.

Chapter IX

We are all part of humanity---each and every one of us. What applies to us also applies to the whole.
The same principles operate for Fear and for Love. Power is to be found in either emotion and each can become an obsession.
Pay mind to which obsession we have chosen to rule your life's processes. Does your essence flow upward, or does it run in a headlong plunge to destruction?
Stop where you are in life and check by which crystal you are empowered.
Take a deep breath, fellow seeker, and name your own personal obsession.
Does it give off the fragrance of life or of death?
Free will is still yours and the choice is in your hands.
A change of thinking will reverse the death cycle in motion. May you choose LIGHT to be your obsession and by doing so, find peace.
All scientists know that to draw a meaningful conclusion, you must have both sides of an effect. You need both negative and positive poles. You must experience the dark and the light for full understanding.
Remember that if negativity is present, then positivity is also present. It is

the Order of the Universe that both negative and positive poles be a part of the whole. This is the Law that keeps all of existence in balance and operating.

Our second crystal is healthy, productive, leading always onward. We are gently encompassed by the warmth of this positive crystal. Its power is felt surging cell to cell but never with heaviness of touch.

Chapter X

    Let us go forward now to explore and to become engrossed in a strange beauty imprisoned just beneath the surface of this crystal. Sparkling, gleaming, shimmering, never still, it suddenly appears in the mind's eye. Never still because always it goes forward---to a goal, a destination. Turning slowly it reveals the glistening white facet of Truth.
    Gazing into the pearlish white essence we stand spellbound as bluish highlights sweep over us with a hypnotic touch. From deep inside, a vision takes form spinning a web of enchantment to enfold us therein. The vision illuminates before us, taking on life and movement. All the spiralling rays of Truth's emotion are exposed. As the mist clears, a lone man stands with hands outstretched for our entry. Behold an Experience....the Obsession of this Man named Christ!
    A shining Truth made Him follow through an incredible, unbelievable giving up of Self. Truth then is obsession when it shines before our eyes and stirs the very strings of our Soul. Truth is obsession when its foundation is strong enough to give it individual identity. Perfection in Truth is achieved when its boundaries are set by wisdom. Truth was a shining star which led the Overseer of this galaxy to complete His guidance task. At the end this Galilean became the very embodiment of His
              Life Purpose.

Momentarily, let us experience some motivating force of a Master Teacher....a Master Teacher who raised the eyes and hearts of humanity. Yes, He raised the eyes of Humanity and they beheld raw, undefiled, and undiluted Truth. They thrilled to truths untouched by human compromise.

Real Truth is a beautiful thing to behold and an unforgettable sight. He opened the hearts of humanity that they might experience the ultimate in Truth application. Truth in any form never comes at one time. We receive a Truth and learn from that thought.

Realization that Christ meant us all to understand is the first Truth. We soon feel the assurance of having access to wonderful powers. The only limitations are self-imposed for our minds may be a gray prison---that chains us to the very mundane things of life. Our thoughts are living, vibrating life forms. The Truth one thinks definitely makes one what one is....moment by moment. Lift up your heart and mind with true thoughts and soar as the eagle far from these limitations.

You will feel the lightness of stepping with the spirit-filled men of old. Your imagination will swell as God's Universal Truths fill every inch of your being. Deep within God's Laws and Miracles gleams the golden, diamond-studded foundation of Truth, built upon the solid ground of Perfect Love. "Greater Things Than These You Will Do In My Name," this Man of Light related to us.

As you really accept Truth and step into the Cosmic River of Love and Understanding, your life will be changed. You will find yourself with hands outstretched to help other souls into the deep warm waters. A voice of unearthly wisdom and love saturates the air, assuring this uncertain soul, "The water's fine....be my guest."

You are amazed to find the voice is yours

and the words form like drops of nectar
in your mind. Suddenly you feel that this
is not your mind at all but a new mind.
   You have opened your tap marked "Universal
Consciousness"....now open, the "waters flow
freely", leaving your mind a beautiful, calm,
serene lake.
   Replenishing its depths daily are the
living springs of life's very core. There
it has been all the time....a golden tap,
and all that was needed to open it was
a Truth.
   Love has created, motivated, and helped
the Universe from the very beginning.
   Behold! that is your Truth---the Truth
that shifted your golden tap into usefulness.
   Love, you say....something so simple.
Love, my friend, has as many facets as a
fallen snowflake and is no simple thing.
Human love is often shallow and changeable
without firm-felt footing. This love we
speak of is our Father's Love. If we could
take the best of man's love and place it
under a powerful microscope---maybe, only
maybe, could we feel a speck of God's love.
Only when we see the vast ocean of love
He spills out for us can we change our own
love capacity. There it is....another Truth,
and the first thing we do is to take on
its vestments. Sharing this raiment of
Truth with others comes as naturally as
breathing. Soon it becomes a legacy and
passes from one to another, growing in power
and warmth. We will find people are brought
to us and the Truth is passed on before
we are aware of it. If we spoke not a
syllable to them, it would still infiltrate
their consciousness like an ever-spreading
flame of golden fire. It leaps from Soul
to Soul. Our paths may never cross again
in this life, but God made sure destiny
brought a brief encounter.

Conceiving and digesting this Truth brings yet another Truth. We soon lose sight of the old fire and brimstone God. In his place is beauty, love, compassion, strength, and power---constantly indwelling in every molecule of this Universe. This God essence loves so perfectly it proposes no horrible punishment such as hell.

Instead, it has allowed us the privilege of working out our own salvation. There it is---still another Truth---Eternal Life in operation. We are allowed to balance out our growth. We polish off the rough edges of this gem life after life, then on a date already set, we return to Him as perfected, pure, shining light.

Our Truth treads upon the heels of another to show the Love and Understanding of this essence of Light. Miracle by miracle will befall our Soul and the chains of the gray prison pass from existence. We could not return to our former state of mind if we wished---one drink from these Universal Waters of Truth and no other waters will quench our thirst. Our vision is fading....leaving understanding of this, our first facet.... in its wake.

Truth

Chapter XI

Our Truth facet rotates out of sight, giving birth to our next concept that moves slowly toward us without the slightest sound. Easing into view is a soft, pink hue of the Love facet. An invitation of warmth is issued forth to our senses. Our second emotional encounter is velvety soft to the touch and filled to the brim with compassion. An aura of strength and calmness gives a glowing radiance as we step carefully into the cushiony interior. Feelings of fulfillment quiet all the physical senses, bringing perfect rhythm and harmony. We feel the overpowering need to give of love. We feel healing will issue forth from the very act of giving love in some form. We must learn to give love so completely that a void is felt in our beings. Then, by all Laws of Nature, the void must be filled. Nothing is ever emptied but that Nature will replace it with an exact complement. This is the great healing mission of Nature in Life's processes.

Love must be given because it is felt to the depths of one's being. Love must be given without any thought of return. Love must be given freely without the want to hear a confirmation of love in return.

The reception of love is not as important as the giving. Your growth comes from the giving, and theirs will come from the receiving of your gift of Love. If the manner of giving is as described, the growth on both sides is perfect. This, then, is what has been glossed over about Love...free, flowing, open without commitment...it must be thus. Your eyes see it, your ears hear it, your emotions feel it, and your Soul knows it is Truth. The fact remains, my friend, it is new ---like a newborn child. Like any birth, pain is present, but the pain leads to enlightenment. Give of Love and it grows, returning to you developed. Again, you give of Love and it smiles, completely enclosing your being with warmth. Still one more time, you extend your Heart and Love, and it shakes the Universe responding back, "I Love You". Serenity flows to your mind whispering, "Be still, Be still!"

Your eyes behold Life with a new quality of perception. Your only measurement of others is on the yardstick of warmth. Sounds of exquisite music fill the air with a new vital movement. It is a Symphony of Love, responding back to you from other spheres of this Universe. Your heart responds and answers, "Yes, that is Love, but not what I know of Love in this Life."

As the music swells and fades in rhythmic sounds, the Soul mimics the beauty therein. Away you climb to heights of inspiration not yet acknowledged by the world at large, free from the limitations of flesh, soaring upward to heaven's full orchestration of Love. Some call it the Song of Life---the Universal Song, which is the essence of all being. It becomes a mirror of your best self. It is there just waiting to be turned loose from the growth pattern of earth.

Pure as light and as real as tomorrow's sunset it exists. You are not alone in your longing for love, peace, and serenity. No, there is an endless tide of souls all filled with a deep need for this type of love. Individually and collectively, they all respond to this rhapsody of life.

All the various instruments of existence quake and tremble to the concerto, you pray, "Grant love to me". Surely the conductor will direct this healing movement to include your empty heart. As he raises his baton, all is poised in readiness to obey the slightest movement. At the dropping of his arm, a Love Overture begins. All is in perfect balance and harmony within this endless rhapsody. Sorrow has done her job and left a clean cavity of emptiness to be filled. Now the time is right with all else in the Universe and it will be done. A new song is offered to you..."A Duet of the Soul".

A river of love flows...filling your sorrow cavity with love of real Nature. Now you give thanks to sorrow and its pain for leaving your heart clean and swept so love may there abide.

You have offered your meditation. You have offered your pleas for love. You have offered your cup to be filled. Now...offer up self.

The house of your true Soul cannot live divided. If self rules supreme, then Love cannot. But with self offered up, Love may live and grow. Love and Self soon merge, becoming one with the Song of Life.

You now find your place in the perfect

rhythm of Creation. Love---real radiating Love---is the most burning form of this puzzlement. When it gives you joy to feel Love, just to feel it---you have an obsession in operation.

Love is obsession when you draw this warmest of emotions to you, only because of your own love capacity. Love's obsession grips you completely and forever when you see its effect in overall splendor...when you look beyond Now to see Love as a beautiful, shining jewel dropped into the Sea of Eternity.

At the point of entry, the circles of effect spread outward with the speed of thought. Enlarging time after time, Love grows and spreads, eventually reaching the fabled shores of Foreverness.

On the return Odyssey, Love experiences rapid growth, becoming a giant, golden sun radiating this highest of emotions. You have, my friend, now become the recipient of something of which you were originally the donor. Your creation has grown at a fantastic rate and returned to you, fully matured.

Real enlightenment comes when you realize that this is the only God-originating emotion we feel. Finally Love becomes obsession when you share it, not keeping it in the confines of a narrow mind.

We feel somewhat as a butterfly emerging from this pink, warm Love cocoon. Our wings are a pageant of pastel colors extending skyward. We actually feel like a new Creation, a Love Creation. We experienced Love in all its emotional splendor. Now we must leave to continue exploration of our crystal. We pause...glancing back at the pink glow. Softly it moves away to make way for the next facet.

Chapter XII

Our attention centers on the everchanging crystal before us...a jaded green infiltrates our minds and our senses. As this portion comes into full view, a pure emerald glow is cast over us. This ever-expending green filament gives the illusion of a flaming desire for growth's procession. Magnificent is this obsession as the mind seeks inspiration, truth, enlightenment, and the freedom to experience. A fire is set ablaze and no manner of trying can extinguish it. Body and mind become only instruments to be used in the business of the Soul. Starting somewhere deep in this pulsating cube of green mist are giant roads. Each road leads off into a different distinct direction. Each direction is a different type of experience growth. All the roads lead onward and upward into a hundred sunrises. Enlightenment of spiritual truth through Life's encounters are the sunrises.

Even though the various roads offer the same end, the routes of achievement are unique to each road and every road. The venture taken on each road is priceless to the Soul's development. Discoveries are numerous, and there are treasures of new things daily. Life, in fact, becomes a treasure hunt, and we become the soldiers of fortunes. Secrets of an eternal nature are the fabled lost cities we seek and find. We explore the ruins, unearthing *golden secrets. These fabled cities release their treasures reluctantly. Therefore, we must be very diligent in our seeking.*

We follow a trail of clues from treasure to treasure. Intuition comes into full play, giving clues and urging us on. Around each bend in the road is yet another discovery, yet another prize.

This world at large becomes our spiritual classroom. For us, a rich bounty lies buried within each and every experience. We have made an excellent discovery since entrance into this Growth facet. There is no hesitation, no stagnation within its concepts. Hesitation gives way to the doubts and fears in life. There is no time within this growth phase for either doubt or fear. Stagnation is the beginning of death.

While the searching for knowledge and truth is the beginning of life, it make no difference if one is on the right, or the wrong, road---the very act of reaching for another step on the Cosmic ladder is what counts. This effort is worth any trouble encountered along the way. Hesitation and stagnation must have inactive ground in order to take root.

Within this portion of our crystal, inactivity is an unheard-of faculty. Not a single inch of space is ever held out for inactivity or boredom. Enlightenment comes as we hold and savour the Landmarks and experiences of life. Throughout all of our travels, there is a strong impression of forward movement which prevails.

Growth can be obtained from all we encounter in life---this becomes fact when our obsessions center in or around the Growth facet. When can growth be considered an obsession or a Life Purpose? Growth is obsession when one is aware that even a moment of time adds to stature...when one understands that each moment has its part to add to growth...when

one understands that both good and bad
experiences add to what we are. Even failure
is a master teacher and adds to knowledge
and growth. Each part, then, makes a whole
in perfect outcome...namely, the Growth
of the Soul.
 The You of Yesterday, Now and Tomorrow
is shaped in growth and progression. Finally,
the inner essence of the Growth obsession is
clear. You understand that it does not matter
which road you choose to travel---they all
center back into the God center. Here rests
the real treasure chest of fabulous, unending
wealth. The beginning and the end of Growth
then circles out of your own higher self.
Growth---no matter what level it approaches
---is perfected within this hidden magic
vault. This is an exciting, stimulating,
questing drive by which we are empowered.
Nothing is so all consuming as an idea, and
the growth portion offers an endless supply
of ideas. Inspiration pours down into thought
form and develops into new ideas. Each day
becomes an adventure filled with miracles.
We live each day of our lives as if it were
the first and the last day to live. Seeing
life this way makes us more aware, detecting
Growth's beauty of work everywhere. We see
more dimensions in all things of Life. Even
a flower extends its past, present and future
to our open consciousness. We relate so
completely, we travel into the very depth
or heart of all we explore in life's journey.
Each relationship takes on three main phases
---Mental, Emotional and Spiritual.
 We experience and learn on all three phases
within the Growth obsession. A feeling of
soft laughter fills this facet to the top
and overflowing. Watch as spontaneous life
erupts from this portion of Growth. This
facet is fed from the springs of healthy
curiosity. Erupting unexpectedly amidst our

thoughts are questions. Each question can lead to a new adventure and another miracle-filled road of discovery.

We feel alive and refreshed---easily responding to new ideas and concepts. Sparks unite here and there as new profitable finds are made known. We watch our thoughts dance about, expelling all fear and all uncertainty.

Blossoms of color burst forth as thoughts grow to full maturity leading to Growth's steps. In shades of a Chinese New Year, the colors shoot skyward. Soon a multi-colored strange beauty takes form before our eyes. The colors slowly fade only to give birth to new explosive thoughts. We are satisfied now with this progressive cubicle. We know the seed of Growth gives birth to the flower of knowledge. Satisfaction is ours as we take leave of this quaking facet. A smile forms its soft folds across our face and we are relieved. It is certain that stagnation and hesitation will never enter here, for the current is too swift and strong. We bid farewell to this positive portion of our exploring venture.

Faith

hope

Chapter XIII

We step with lightness into the next facet called Faith and Hope. Greeting us upon entrance are all the uplifting emotions of great expectations. Confidence reigns supreme master within these fluorescent walls. Found here is downy, soft clouds of fulfilled wishes and dreams realized. Here, to ask for is to receive from a Universal Source of abundance. The act of asking is not even necessary for we know all will be supplied should the need be physical, mental or spiritual---the supply essence never changes.

Whisps of color take form in unique patterns in intricate shapes before us. First, violet runs a gambit of shades manifesting Faith. It starts with soft violet and extends into a brilliant pageant of royal purples. The orange tones of glowing Hope forming nearby, are given life. Mental yellows spin and swirl, merging with the hopeful golden shades. The deep orange of the sun takes a positive potent position of health giving power. They form and reform, merging and swirling together---taking on awareness of the unseen processes which are the fabled magic lamp.

No grieving for yesterday delivers up mournful cries here, no sadness for past mistakes is given an audience, no wishing away today, no hurrying tomorrow. Worry cannot build its prison walls for Faith and Hope are in full command. They man a mighty fortress built upon a rock of universal supply. Depression never steals a single precious moment of time, nor darkness a single corner. Never present are these wasters of human time, emotions, and energy. Never is sanity threatened by these **pestilents** of the human race.

   The chamber of Faith and Hope play host to the higher levels of cause and effect. To think is to make manifest. Tomorrow's state of affairs already exists. We find contentment in whatever state we are. This delightful chamber of miracles exists in each and every soul. This part of our Power crystal can be set into motion by the Soul through the Mind. What a very special and perfect way to give order to life. We know a return visit here would be a very welcome experience, almost an excursion of a delightful, delicate existence.

   Feelings of a strange Shangri-La floats to us upon leaving. Yes, the chamber really is the mystical Shangri-La of the Mind. A Shangri-La where time takes on a new meaning, where all things exist now and tomorrow, where dimensions are crossed without a moment's hesitation, where the beauty of life never withers and never disappears, where channels are open wide to the Universe at large...We feel protected here and enclosed in the warmth of
assurance.

   Time for our departure is now upon us and we reluctantly retreat. Glancing back, we feel a return visit is certainly in order. Already our mind speeds ahead, planning a return to this wonderladen, timeless space.

Chapter XIV

Instantly, the drawing force of the next facet is upon us. Beauty sends out her serene song persuading us to enter her facet. Our dazed eyes move quickly over the exterior. A shiny, silvery radiance beyond belief fills this aspect of our crystal. Speak about the loveliness of Life...Speak about the beauty of the world and life...yet we know not of Real Beauty---the real basic beauty that indwells and encases all things. Think not of the normal range of beauty usually encountered---look into everything for the form of beauty existing in all creation.

A universal undercurrent flows in the very depths forming a special beauty. Real beauty is to feel and to see the universe in perfect rhythmic flow, to look deep and see the ebb and flow of life in a glorious arrangement of color. As the universe flows, it spreads its peacock feathers---shading upon shading extends forth, taking on new form moment to moment. Our breath is stilled as beauty's fullness suppresses all human efforts. Now beauty is lengthening, reaching, extending, and spreading its light. Harmony soothes all as soft pastel colors ebb in graceful retreat.

Again and again the rich sharp cascade of color flows, only to ebb with soft pastels. Color becomes all life in expressive action and reaction. We become the artist comprehending the beauty of all things to new eyes. The senses are heightened,

*receiving worlds of beauty's revelations.
Breathtaking sights are displayed on all
sides. Life responds in depth after depth
of Beauty. Worlds within worlds are open
to the mind. The mind opens new horizons
within its own physical capacity. Unused
portions of the mind take on life to
enable us more Beauty conception.*

*We feel light as our mind extends in
new growth. Loveliness pervades all life
and extends into every cell of being. We
breath slowly, quietly, effortlessly---
taking in Life's very core. What beauty we
find at this encounter level! Creation is
giving birth from this magnificent life bud.
The ebb and flow here are Life-forming,
Life-giving, Life-receiving. Glowing just a
touch away is Life in Perfect Order, Life
in Divine Order. Like a magnificent giant
breathing life, is this creating process.*

*Life's system flows outward to return
from whence it came. The endless system in
timeless perfection is Perfect Beauty,
Perfect Order, Perfect Form. Color here
never stays the same moment to moment. It
changes constantly, always forming the new,
always in the process of becoming or
creating. We for the first time, see the
real Beauty of Life as Perfect Order.*

*We are lifted gently from the center of
all and placed in space. Here we gaze upon
this lovely crystal of Positive Perfect Good.
We are moved out at a distance to ponder the
positive results of analysis. Our gem
continues in motion and we can observe
countless divisions. They are all shades
and tints of the main facets just entered.
There is no argument as to the worth of the
positive obsession of mankind, nor the
beauty encountered there.*

Chapter XV

*There is only one more Supreme Positive State to enter and experience; however, this state of Consciousness is a result of application of all the positive facets together. We could not stand to experience the feelings all at one time; therefore, we shall enter the Christ Consciousness in stages. Does it sound and seem the **impossible** state of Consciousness to achieve? Christ Consciousness is a sleeping, potent seed within all of Creation. By the application of the Positive Obsession, or the Positive Life Purposes, this state can be achieved.*

The whole powerful crystal used together waters this seed of Christ Consciousness in us. Soon healthy life spreads forth, releasing the facet of the ultimate state. We enter upon the first stage with the feeling of expansion. An essence of golden sun colors this phase of Consciousness. The mind extends, yields, comprehends, and realizes the Truth. Here we are...not as we are, but as we hope to be. The image of what is to come is all within the Seed of Life ---that potent portion called Soul.

A hugh vintage is contained in a small seed. The concept of a man is contained within the womb of Life, so the image of our Soul's Growth is contained in the

*seed of the Christ Consciousness. Both
the beginning and the end are pictured
within our Christ-conscious seed. Framed
within Life's endless revelations and
timeless limits exists Creation. Image
after image takes form within this
picture giving it Life. In active
movement---changing, reforming, it is
an enigma, yet no matter what form is
present, it encompasses the same qualities
and quantities of Consciousness. Always
this picture is in a state of being
complete in a form chosen at the
moment. In whatever pattern of existence
we choose, it is complete. We come to the
place where we relate to this Creating
Movement Process. We then become
ourselves in a process of directional
Creation. Time after time, we become
the Creator and we are the Creation.
These activities and processes are
unseen and unfelt, but certainly span
existence.*

  *We soon learn to salute the Christ
Consciousness in others. The ability to
see beyond the flesh image of man
becomes habit---swept away is all
prejudice and judging of another. We
know without a doubt that in each face
we behold a mirror. This mirror reflects
the two natures within them and us.
One nature is displayed in the Physical
Laws of Cause and Effect. The second
higher nature is displayed in Christ
Consciousness. Divine Law and Divine
Love operates here, giving birth to
Perfect Soul Union.*

  *· Slowly, it becomes obvious that we
set this stage out of reach ourselves.
In reality, this is a needless
separation and not meant to be. This
power of Consciousness is given to us*

from every atom and molecule. Direct is the connection with all else in Creation. We make our own blocks to this state with our minds and ego. No door exists between us and the Creative Spirit. It is around us, through us, and of us. It is acting, reacting, and becoming one in the same.

The mind clears and we understand the simplicity, the basic truth of it all. The same creative force in operation at the beginning is in operation now. Never does Creation stop and we are all a part of this Creative Mind. Eternity started at Point Zero and extends to Point Zero within the Universal Circle of Time.

In this state of Consciousness, we know Truth's light and feel Love's warmth, see Beauty's undercurrent, experience expansive Growth and are then at rest. The love felt in this state is the rarest of Loves, completing our Soul's magnitude.

Our Soul seems to soar beyond the self-imposed limitations. The infinite compassion of this state encompasses our Being completely. We are cradled tenderly and shielded within this concept. This portion of one's Soul is a gift of Love from an all-knowing, all-loving God essence. This promise of completeness is long in coming but stands the test of time.

Yes, now is the time---the time to claim fulfillment. Each Soul shows the scars of a Life of searching for this state of Consciousness. The reality of this condition had led us as a beacon in the darkest hours. Observe this Life as charted by the stars and each one of us is a Soul with a mission. The mission is to shed some Light into this world. What kind of Light do we speak of? The Light of Truth, the Truth of our Origin, and the Truth of the Love force that spun us into existence. The Truth of Universal kinship which is deep and full within all of us. At this state of Consciousness, we are assured of the strength to complete this mission of Love. With completion, we then can bathe in the Light and Truth of Peace.

Protection surrounds us in the presence of the warm assurance of real Love. As we empty our cup of Love in this state of Comprehension, a flowing river of warmth returns to us. We realize this union is a miniature picture of the final union with the God head.

Now we feel the chains of karmic necessity dropping from us. The freedom of spontaneous uplifting Soul Love moves in like a cloud of pure joy. The desparate tugs of responsibility from other dimensions give way to the recognition of this state. All the strength and answers are within and available. This then is the pure picture of Spiritual Union and the true Spiritual Rebirth.

We now feel, act, and think no longer as before. A deeper sense of appreciation of all things spreads relentlessly to every fiber of our being. The normal senses of the body are heightened to a state of painful sensitivity. The unseen senses of our Souls are allowed prominence over the mundane. Then we radiate...we experience the ultimate emotion of pure Love.

We are surprised to find anger is no longer possible. What hurts another is our pain, also. Sadness for others brings tears of compassion to our eyes. Joy and happiness for others brings *ecstatic joy to our hearts*. Injustice in the world brings sorrow to our bosom. We find, for the very first time, we love wholly without a thought for self. Just the image of this state brings such a full ecstasy it spills over and infects all we touch with a Christ-like spirit. All we touch from this point of rebirth will never be the same again. All will be changed by the Love Fountain which flows and bubbles within us.

The Soul has spent this life much as an alien in a foreign country. Deep in the recesses of our Being was the feeling of imperfection, much like an unfinished painting, or a song without music. Now, it is as if the master composer bends low over his work finishing his concerto with perfection.

With the beauty of the completed masterpiece, we are ready to serve our Purpose in Life. Nothing of the Universe is hidden from our eyes. All is in a grand display inviting inspection. Our mind is a new mind and sends out new sensations into the furthest fathoms of this Universal ocean. Thoughts fill the air in a Love conversation with all of Creation and says, "Build me an altar deep in the Valley of my Soul that I might give thanks daily for God's pattern so perfect it even takes care of one lonely Soul. Make my eyes see and know the beauty of the unlovely things of the Universe."

We have a new insight into God's

purpose for all encountered in Life's pilgrimage. The Soul experiences, extends, and includes every other individual touched. The effect lasts until the Soul eventually wings its way from Earth's bondage. Continually this becomes our conversation and prayer. All fibers of being are included in the thought processes. This Soul consciousness has heightened even this part of our awareness. Freedom to converse with the Universe at large is available and so automatically is the Power, Love, Glory, and Beauty of a timeless, limitless Cosmos. You together with this state of Universal consciousness, exist more in the higher plains than on earth. There is nothing---absolutely nothing---one cannot accomplish while in this Union of Self. We have now experienced the ultimate in the positive Consciousness of Man. We have travelled the length and width of the Positive Obsession.

It is my prayer and my belief that having read this offering, you will never be the same again. Never will you narrow your Soul to the limitations of your Mind. You have visited Man in his self-made Hell and you have soared with him to his ecstasies in Heaven. You have seen Man in utter darkness and beheld Man in blinding light. You have seen the magnificent Creature called Christ in You.

DARE YOU EVER LOSE SIGHT OF THIS IMAGE OF
REAL LIFE!

Love

Lobe

ARIES PRESS PUBLICATIONS

A-P Table of Houses - to 66° North Latitude
  Latitudes of major cities throughout the world

Degrees of the Zodiac Symbolized
        Alan Leo

Calculator Key to Astrology
        Juliann

How to Use the Modern Ephemeris
        Elbert Benjamine

The Mysteries of Color
        John Sandbach

The Golden Cycle, a Text on the Tarot
        John Sandbach & Ronn Ballard

I Ching Primer and Oracle Pad
        Frank R. Kegan

Instant Oracle
        Frank R. Kegan

Oracle Book
        Frank R. Kegan

April 4, 1981, Pivotal Day in a Critical Year
        Jim Gross et al

Stars & Stoves, an Astrological Cookbook
        Barbara Morbidoni

Aries Press Journal, the New Age Anthology
                and
Astro-Discs, plastic templates in 4 diameters

Cover Design and Calligraphy by

Sonja Foxe
Chicago